Impressum
Verlag: BABADADA GmbH, Nedderfeld 112 , 22529 Hamburg
Geschäftsführer / Verlagsleitung: Harald Hof
Druck: Books on Demand GmbH, In de Tarpen 42, 22848 Norderstedt

Imprint
Publisher: BABADADA GmbH, Nedderfeld 112 , 22529 Hamburg, Germany
Managing Director / Publishing direction: Harald Hof
Print: Books on Demand GmbH, In de Tarpen 42, 22848 Norderstedt

classroom
القسم

divide
يقسم

186/2

board
لوحة

school yard
لاكور

teacher
معلم

paper
ورقة

write
يكتب

pen
ستيلو

desk
بيرو

ruler
مسطرة

book
كتاب

pupil
تلميذ

satchel

كرطاب

pencil case

المقلمة

pencil

قلم الرصاص

pencil sharpener

منجارة

rubber

ممحا

drawing pad

الكايي تاع الرسم

drawing

الرسم

paintbrush

البانسو

paint box

باتير

scissors

مقص

glue

كولا

exercise book

كايي تاع التمارين

homework

الواجبات

number

النيميرو

add

يجمع

subtract

يطرح

multiply

يضرب

calculate

يحسب

letter

الحرف

alphabet

الحروف

word

كلمة

text

النص

read

يقرا

chalk

طباشير

lesson

الدرس

register

دفتر المدرسي

examination

ليقزاما

certificate

سرتفيكا

school uniform

ليكول تاع اللبة

education

التعليم

encyclopedia

ليكسيك

university

الجاميعة

microscope

المجهر

map

الخريطة

waste-paper basket

بوبال

hotel
اوتال

hostel
بيت الشباب

ROOMS

currency exchange office
بيرة تاع الصرف

EXCHANGE

suitcase
فاليزة

car
لولو

language
اللغة ليقصدها

yes / no
واه / لا

Okay
صحا

hello
مرحبا

translator
طرجمان

Thank you
صحيت

how much is...?

شحال السومة؟

I don´t get it

مفهمتش

problem

مشكيلة

Good evening!

مسلخير

Good morning!

صباح لخير

Good night!

تصبح بخير

goodbye

بسلامة

direction

ديركسيو

luggage

الباقاج

bag

ساك

backpack

ساكادو

guest

ضيف

room

شمبرا

sleeping bag

ساك تاع رقاد

tent

خيمة

tourist information

استعلامات سياحية

beach

بجر

credit card

كارطة ناع الكريدي

breakfast

فطور الصباح

lunch

الفطور

dinner

العشا

Ticket

البيي

elevator

امونسير

stamp

تامير

border

الحدود

customs

الديوانة

embassy

سقارة

visa

فيزا

passport

باسبور

airplane
طيارة

ship
بابور

fire truck
لبونيبا

truck
كاميونة

bus
بيس

motorboat
بوطي

car
لولو

bike
بيسكلات

ferry

بابو

boat

بوطي

motorbike

موطو

police car

لوطو تاع لابوليس

racing car

لوطو تاع السيباق

rental car

لوطو تاع كرية

car sharing

لواطا تاع كرية

tow truck

رومورك

garbage truck

كاميو تاع الزبل

engine

موتور

fuel

ليسونس

fuel station

ستاسيون

traffic sign

بانو

traffic

ترافيك

traffic jam

سركالة

parking lot

باركينغ

train station

لاقار

tracks

السبيكة

train

قطار

tram

ترام

wagon

فاغون

helicopter

الهليكوبتر

airport

مطار

tower

تور

passenger

مسافر

container

كونتنار

carton

كرطونة

cart

شاريو

basket

سلة

take off / land

يقلع / يهود

city

مان

village

قرية

city center

البلاد

house

دار

![City scene illustration with labels]

- movie theater — سينما
- advert — لا بيب
- street light — اضرا عاتا ضوصلا
- street — طريق
- taxi — طاكسى
- snack shop — كيوسك
- pedestrian — بييطون
- sidewalk — عاطورت
- zebra crossing — نوتيبي جاسب
- dumpster — بويال
- crossing — نوبنر
- traffic lights — جوريف

hut

كوخ

apartment

برطمان

train station

لاقار

city hall

لاميري

museum

متحف

school

ليكول

university

الجامعة

bank

بانكة

hospital

سبيطار

hotel

اوتال

pharmacy

فارماسي

office

بيرو

book shop

مكتبة

shop

حانوت

flower shop

فلوريست

supermarket

سوبرات

market

مرشي

department store

حانوت كبير

fishmonger's shop

مسمكة

mall

سونتر كومرسيال

harbor

المينا

park

بارك

bench

بنك

bridge

جسر

stairs

درج

subway

ميترو

tunnel

تونال

bus stop

لاري تاع البيس

bar

بار

restaurant

مطعم

postbox

صندوق البريد

street sign

البانوات

parking meter

مقياس زمن الوقوف

zoo

حديقة حيوانات

swimming pool

بيسين

mosque

جامع

farm

فيرما

pollution

التلوث

cemetery

مقبرة

church

قليزية

playground

بارك

temple

معبد

landscape

الريف

leaf
ورقة

signpost
بانو

path
طريق

meadow
مرج

stone
حجرة

hiker
رحالة

tree
شجرة

river
نهر

grass
حشيش

flower
زهرة

valley

واد

hill

جبل

lake

بحيرة

forest

غابة

desert

صحرا

volcano

بركان

castle

شاطو

rainbow

قوس قزح

mushroom

فطر

palm tree

نخلة

mosquito

ناموسة

fly

ذبابة

ant

نملة

bee

نحلة

spider

رتيلة

beetle

خنفوس

frog

جرانة

squirrel

سنجاب

hedgehog

قنفود

hare

قنينة

owl

بومة

bird

زاوش

swan

بجعة

boar

حلوف

deer

عزالة

moose

إلكة

dam

سد

wind turbine

الطاحونة

solar panel

خلية شمسية

climate

كليما

waiter
سارفور

menu
المونيو

chair
كرسي

soup
سوية

pizza
بيتزا

cutlery
كوفار

tablecloth
ناب

starter
اوردوفر

main course
الطبق الرئيسي

dessert
ديسار

drinks
مشروبات

food
ماكلة

bottle
القرعة

fast food

فاست فود

street food

ماكلة نديه معايا

teapot

براد اتاي

sugar bowl

سكرية

portion

طرف

espresso machine

ماشينة تاع اكسبريسو

high chair

كرسي عالي

bill

فاتورة

tray

سني

knife

خدمي

fork

فرشيطة

spoon

مغيرفة

teaspoon

مغيرفة تاع لاتاي

serviette

سربيتة تاع الطابلة

glass

كاس

plate

طبسي

soup plate

بول

saucer

طبسي تاع الفنجال

sauce

لاصوص

salt shaker

القوطي تاع الملح

pepper mill

طحان تاع الحرور

vinegar

خل

oil

زيت

spices

ليزيبيس

ketchup

كتشوب

mustard

موطارد

mayonnaise

مايونيز

special offer
برومسيو

customer
كلويون

dairy products
مشتقات الحليب

FOR

fruit
فاكية

shopping cart
شاريو

butcher's shop

بوشي

bakery

بولونجي

weigh

يوزن

vegetables

خضار

meat

لحم

frozen food

سيرجولي

cold cuts

كاشير

canned food

كونسارف

detergent

الاومو تاع لغسيل

candy

الحلويات

household products

صوالح الدار

cleaning products

ديتارجو

sales representative

فوندوز / خدامة فالحانوت

cash register

لاكاس

cashier

كاسسي

shopping list

ليستا تاع الشري

opening hours

سوايع الخدمة

wallet

تزرداتم

credit card

كارطة ناع الكريدي

bag

ساك

plastic bag

بورسة

water

الماء

juice

جو

milk

حليب

coke

كوكا

wine

الشراب

beer

البيرة

alcohol

شراب

cocoa

كاكاو

tea

لاتناي

coffee

قهوة

espresso

اكسبريسو

cappuccino

كابوتشينو

banana

بانانة

apple

تفاح

orange

تشينا

melon

بطيخ

lemon

ليم

carrot

كروطة / زرودية

garlic

ثوم

bamboo

بانبو

onion

بصل

mushroom

شانبينيو

nuts

بندق

noodles

ليبات

spaghetti

سباقيتي

rice

روز

salad

سلاطة

fries

ليفريت

fried potatoes

ليفريت

pizza

بيتزا

hamburger

هانبورقر

sandwich

سندويش

escalope

اسكالوب

ham

لحم الحلوف

salami

سامي

sausage

مرقاز

chicken

جاجة

roast

لحم مشوي

fish

حوت

porridge oats

شوفان

muesli

موسلي

cornflakes

كورن فلكس

flour

فرينة

croissant

كرواسون

bread roll

خبيزة

bread

الخبز / كسرة

toast

خبز محمر

cookies

بيسكوي

butter

زبدة

curd

لبن

cake

قاطو

egg

بيض

fried egg

بيض مقلي

cheese

فرماج

ice cream

لاكرام

sugar

سكر

honey

عسل

jelly

كونفتير

nougat cream

نوقا

curry

الكاري

farm house
فيرمة

straw bale
رزمة تاع تبن

barn
مخزن

field
حقل

horse
عود

trailer
قنطرة

foal
مهر

tractor
جرار

donkey
حمار

lamb
خروف

sheep
كبش

goat

معزة

cow

بقرة

calf

عجل

pig

حلوف

piglet

حلوف صغير

bull

طورو

goose

وِزَة

duck

بَطَة

chick

فِلْوُس

hen

جَاجَة

cockerel

كُودْرَس

rat

بَوْطا

cat

قِطَة

mouse

فَأْر

ox

ثَوْر

dog

كَلْب

dog house

دَار الْكَلْب

garden hose

يُوبِيت

watering can

إِبْرِيق

scythe

مِنْجَل

plow

مِحْرَاث

sickle

منجل

hoe

الفاس

pitchfork

مذراة الزبل

axe

شاقور

pushcart

برويطة

trough

معلف

milk can

قابة تاع حليب

sack

ساشيا

fence

سياج

stable

صطبل

greenhouse

بوطاجي

soil

تراب

seed

بذور

fertilizer

سماد

combine harvester

حصادة

harvest

يحصد

harvest

الغلة

yams

بطاط

wheat

قمح

soya

صويا

potato

بطاطا

corn

ماييس

rapeseed

سلجم

fruit tree

شجرة تاع فاكية

manioc

منيهوت

grain

الخبوب

chimney
شوميني

roof
سقّف

downspout
بالة

window
ناقة

garage
قاراج

doorbell
صونات

door
باب

trash can
بوبال

mailbox
بواطة تاع البرية

garden
جاردان

living room

صالون

bathroom

الحمام

kitchen

كوزينا

bedroom

داق تاع ابرماش

kids room

يراري تاع ابرميش

dining room

صالة مونجي

floor

لرض

wall

حيط

ceiling

بلافو

cellar

كافا

sauna

سونا

balcony

بالكون

terrace

تيراسة

pool

بيسين

lawn mower

جزارة تاع حشيش

sheet

ساووا

bedspread

كووات

bed

ناموسية

broom

مصلحة

bucket

بيدو تاع صليح

switch

انتغبتور

wallpaper
ورق تاع حيطان

picture
تصويرة

lamp
لامبا

shelf
ايتجار

cabinet
بلاكار

television
تيليفزيون

fireplace
شوميني

flower
زهرة

cushion
مخدة

vase
فاز

sofa
صافا

remote control
تيليكومند

carpet

طابي

drape

ريدو

table

طابلة

chair

كرسي

rocking chair

كرسي يبوجي

armchair

فوتاي

book

كتاب

blanket

طوفيرطة

decoration

زواق

firewood

الحطب

film

فيلم

stereo system

الستيريو

key

مفتاح

newspaper

جرنان

painting

كادر

poster

بوستار

radio

راديو

notebook

كناش

vacuum cleaner

اسبيراتور

cactus

صبار

candle

شمعة

fridge
فريجو

microwave oven
ميكرريند

kitchen scales
ميزان تاع الكوزينة

toaster
غريبان

laundry detergent
ديترجون

stove
فورتو

freezer
فريجيدان

trash can
بوبال

dishwasher
غسالة تاع ماعين

cooker

الفور

pot

قدرة

cast-iron pot

مرميطا

wok / kadai

طاوة غامقة

pan

مقلة

kettle

غلاية

steamer

قدرة

baking tray

سني

crockery

ماعين

mug

قوبلي

bowl

طبسي

chopsticks

مطارق تاع الماكلة

ladle

لوشة

spatula

سباتولة

whisk

الضرابة

strainer

كسكاس

sieve

صفاية

grater

راب

mortar

مهراز

barbecue

شواية

fireplace

موقد

chopping board

بلونشا

rolling pin

رولو

corkscrew

الحلال

can

قابسة

can opener

الحلال

oven cloth

كتان

sink

لافابو

brush

بروسة

sponge

بونجة

blender

الخلاط

deep freezer

فريغو

baby bottle

بيبرونة

tap

سبالة

heating
شوفاج

shower
دوش

towel
سريتة

shower curtain
شادو تاع ريدو

bubble bath
حمام بالرغوة

bathtub
بنوار

washing machine
غسالة تاع حوايج

glass
كاس

tap
سبالة

tiles
كرلاج

potty
ليو

sink
لافابو

toilet

توالات

squat toilet

توالات تركي

bidet

غسال الرجلين

urinal

مبولة

toilet paper

ورق تاع توالات

toilet brush

بروسة تاع توالات

toothbrush

بروسدون

toothpaste

دونتقريس

dental floss

خيط السنان

wash

يغسل

hand shower

دوشات تاع دوش

douche

دوشات

basin

لافابو

back brush

بروسا تاع الظهر

soap

صابون

shower gel

جال دوش

shampoo

شنبوان

flannel

الحبل

drain

قادوس

creme

بومادة

deodorant

ديودورون

mirror

مراية

hand mirror

مراة صغيرة

razor

رازوار

shaving foam

لاموس

aftershave

كولون

comb

مشطة

brush

بروسة

hair-dryer

سشوار

hairspray

مثبت الشعر

makeup

مكياج

lipstick

روجالافر

nail varnish

فرني

cotton wool

قطن

nail scissors

كوبينغل

perfume

ريحة

washbag

تروسة تاع حمام

stool

طابوري

weighing scales

ميزان

bathrobe

بينوار

rubber gloves

ليغونات تاع النيتواياج

tampon

تمبون

sanitary towel

ليبيوند

chemical toilet

توالات

alarm clock
ريڨاي

cuddly toy
نونورس

toy car
لوطو جوري

rattle
الخشخاش

doll's house
دار تاع بوبيات

present
كادو

balloon

بالونة / نسافة

bed

ناموسية

stroller

بوسات

deck of cards

الكارطة

jigsaw

البوزيل

comic

بوند ديسيني

lego bricks

الليغو

toy blocks

حجر يينوه

action figure

بوبية

romper suit

لبسة تاع البيبي

frisbee

فريزي

mobile

اللهاية

board game

لعبة الطابلة

dice

الدي

model train set

التران

pacifier

سوسات

party

حفلة / الفيشطة

picture book

كتاب بتصاوير

ball

بالون

doll

بوبية

play

يلعب

sandpit

بارك بالرملة

swing

بنصوار

toys

جوي

video game console

منيطا

tricycle

بيسكلات

teddy bear

دبدوب

wardrobe

ماريو

clothing

حوايج

socks

تقاشر

stockings

ليبيا

tights

كولو

scarf
شال

umbrella
بربلوي

t-shirt
تريكو

belt
حزام

boots
بوط

slippers
بنتوفلا

sneakers
تينيسا / سبردينا

sandals

صندالة

shoes

صباط

rubber boots

بوط بلاستيك

underwear

كالسون

bra

سوتيان

undershirt

حويج تاع داخل

body

لاسق على الجسم

pants

سروال

jeans

جين

skirt

جيبا

blouse

طابلية

shirt

قمجة

pullover

تريكو

sweater

قارديقون

blazer

بلازار

jacket

فيستا

coat

بالطو

raincoat

بالطو

costume

كوستيم

dress

روبا

wedding dress

شنبلون روب

suit

كوستيم

nightgown

شوميز دونوي

pajamas

بيجاما

sari

ساري

headscarf

حجاب

turban

عمامة

burka

برقع

kaftan

قفطان

abaya

عباية

swimsuit

مايو

trunks

سروال تاع عوم

shorts

شورت

tracksuit

لبسة تاع سبور

apron

طابلية

gloves

ليقونات

button

قفلة

glasses

نواظر

bracelet

براسلي

necklace

سنسلة

ring

خاتم

earring

منقوش

cap

بوني

coat hanger

سانتر

hat

شابو

tie

قرافاطة

zip

غيمة

helmet

كاسك

braces

بروتال

school uniform

اللبة تاع ليكول

uniform

لينيفورم

bib

رياقة

pacifier

سوسات

diaper

ليكوش

server
سارفر

filing cabinet
خزانة تاع الملفات

printer
امبريمائت

paper
ورقة

monitor
ليكرون

desk
بيرو

mouse
لاسوري

folder
كلاسور

keyboard
كلافيي

waste-paper basket
بوبال

chair
كرسي

computer
اوردينائور

coffee mug

كاس قهوة

calculator

كاكولاتريس

internet

لانترنت

laptop

اورديناتور

letter

برية

message

ميساج

cell phone

بورطابل

network

ريزو

photocopier

فوطوكوبي

software

لوجسيال

telephone

تيلفون

plug socket

بريزة

fax machine

فاكس

form

استمارة

document

وثيقة

buy

يشري

pay

يخلص

trade

يتاجر

money

دراهم

dollar

دولار

euro

اورو

yen

ين

rouble

روبل

Swiss franc

فرنك سويسري

renminbi yuan

يوان

rupee

روبية

cash point

ديستريبيتّور

currency exchange office

بيرة تاع الصرف

gold

ذهب

silver

فضة

oil

نفط

energy

طاقة

price

السومة

contract

عقد

tax

طاكس

stock

سهم

work

يخدم

employee

خدام

employer

مول الشي

factory

وزين

shop

حانوت

police officer
بوليسي

fireman
بومبي

pilot
بيلوط

doctor
الطبيب

cook
طباخ

gardener

جرديني

carpenter

نجار

seamstress

خياط

judge

قاضي

chemist

شيميك

actor

ممثل

bus driver

شوفير

taxi driver

طاكسيور

fisherman

صياد

cleaning lady

خدامة

roofer

ماصو تاع الصقف

waiter

سارفور

hunter

صياد

painter

بنتار

baker

خباز

electrician

الكتريسيان

builder

ماصون

engineer

مهندس

butcher

بوشي

plumber

بلومبي

postman

فاكتور

soldier

جندي

architect

ارشيتكت

cashier

كاسسي

florist

بياع اورد

hairdresser

كوافير

conductor

الكنترول

mechanic

ميكانيسيان

captain

كابيتان

dentist

طبيب سنان

scientist

عالم

rabbi

حاخام

imam

امام

monk

موان

pastor

موان

hammer
مارطو

pliers
كلاب

screwdriver
تورنفيس

wrench
مفتاح

torch
تورشا

excavator

جرافة

toolbox

قايصة نتاع ليزوتي

ladder

سلوم

saw

منشار

nails

مسامير

drill

برسوز

repair

يصنع

shovel

البالة

Damn!

ياويلي

dustpan

بالا

paint can

بو تاع بنتورة

screws

ليفيس

musical instruments

آلات موسيقية

drum set
آلات الإيقاع

loud speaker
مكبر الصوت

guitar
غيتارة

double bass
كمان أجهر

trumpet
بوق

piano

بيانو

violin

كمنجة

bass

جهير

timpani

طبل كبير

drums

طبل

keyboard

بيانو كهربائي

saxophone

ساكسوفون

flute

ناي

microphone

ميكروفون

entrance
المدخلة

tiger
نمر

cage
كاجا

zebra
حمار الوحش

animal feed
علف للحيوانات

panda
باندا

animals

حيوانات

elephant

فيل

kangaroo

كنغر

rhino

وحيد القرن

gorilla

غوريلا

bear

دب

camel

جمل

ostrich

نعامة

lion

سبع

monkey

نشيطا

flamingo

فلامونغوز

parrot

بيروكي

polar bear

دب قطبي

penguin

بطريق

shark

سمك القرش

peacock

طاووس

snake

لفعة

crocodile

تمساح

zookeeper

عساس في حديقة الحيوان

seal

عجل البحر

jaguar

نمر أمريكي مرقط

pony

فرس قزم

leopard

نمر

hippo

فرس النهر

giraffe

زرافة

eagle

نسر

boar

حلوف

fish

حوت

turtle

فكرون

walrus

حيوان فظ البحري

fox

ثعلب

gazelle

غزال

American football
بالون اميريكا

cycling
الركبة تاع البيسكلت

tennis
تينيس

basketball
باسكات

swimming
العوم

boxing
بوكس

ice hockey
هوكي

soccer

بالون

badminton

الريشة الطائرة

athletics

اتلاتيزم

handball

الهوند

skiing

سكي

polo

بولو

laugh
يضحك

jump
ينقز

hug
يعنق

walk
يمشي

sing
يغني

dream
ينوم

pray
يصلي

kiss
يبوس

write
يكتب

draw
يرسم

show
يوري

push
يدمر

give
يعطي

take
يدي

have

يملك

do

يخدم

be

كاين

stand

يوقف

run

يجري

pull

يجبد

throw

يقيس / يرمي

fall

يطيح

lie

يتكسل

wait

يشوف

carry

يرفد

sit

يقعد

get dressed

يلبس

sleep

يرقد

wake up

ينوط

look at

يشوف في

cry

يبكي

stroke

يحك

comb

يمشّط

talk

يهدر

understand

يفهم

ask

يسقسي

listen

يسمع

drink

يشرب

eat

ياكل

tidy up

يخمل

love

يبغي

cook

يطيب

drive

يصوق

fly

يطير

sail

 يبحر بالفلوكة

calculate

يحسب

read

يقرا

learn

يتعلم

work

يخدم

marry

يتزوج

sew

يخيط

brush teeth

يغسل سنانو

kill

يكتل

smoke

يكمي

send

يرسل

grandmother
الجدة

grandfather
الجد

father
الأب

mother
الأم

baby
الذري

daughter
البنت

son
الولد

guest

ضيف

aunt

العمة / الخالة

uncle

العم / الخال

brother

الخو

sister

الخت

forehead
الجبهة

eye
العين

shoulder
الكتف

finger
صبع

face
الوجه

chin
اللحية

hand
اليد

breast
الصدر

leg
الساق

arm
الذراع

baby

الذري

man

الراجل

woman

المرا

girl

الشيرة، الطفلة

boy

الشير

head

الراس

back

ظهر

belly

الكرش

navel

السرة

toe

صبع

heel

طالون

bone

العظم

hip

المرادف

knee

الركبة

elbow

لمرفغ

nose

نيف

buttocks

مصاصيط

skin

البشرة

cheek

الحنوك

ear

لوذن

lip

شورب

mouth

الفم

tooth

السنة

tongue

اللسان

brain

الدماغ

heart

القلب

muscle

العضلة

lung

الرية

liver

الكبدة

stomach

لسطوما

kidneys

كلوى

sex

رابور

condom

فيتيفرازيرب

ovum

البويضة

semen

سيرم

pregnancy

شركلب

menstruation

غرايل

vagina

المهبل

penis

المذاكر

eyebrow

الحاجب

hair

الشعر

neck

رقبة

body - الجسم

71

hospital
سبيطار

ambulance
لانبيلونس

wheelchair
الكرسي المتحرك

fracture
فاتورة

doctor

الطبيب

emergency room

ليزيرجونس

nurse

الممرضة

emergency

ليرجونس

unconscious

تغاشى

pain

الوجع

injury

الجرح

bleeding

يسيل الدم

heart attack

القلب

stroke

لافيسي

allergy

لالرجي

cough

الكحة

fever

الحمة

flu

لاقريب

diarrhea

الاسهال

headache

ميغران

cancer

السرطان

diabetes

السكر

surgeon

الجراح

scalpel

مبضع

operation

عملية تاع القلب

CT

لاسيتي

x-ray

الراديو

ultrasound

لولتخازرون

face mask

لماسك

disease

المرض

waiting room

وين يقارعو

crutch

العكاز

plaster

سكوتش

bandage

لبانسما

injection

ليرة

stethoscope

السماعة تاع الطبيب

stretcher

نقالة

clinical thermometer

لوزنو بيه الحمة

birth

زيادة

overweight

السمونية

hearing aid

جهاز السمع

disinfectant

المعقم

infection

لنفكسون

virus

الفيروس

HIV / AIDS

السيدا

medicine

الدوا

vaccination

الفاكسان

tablets

الدوا حب

pill

بيلولة

emergency call

يعيط للنجدة

blood pressure monitor

الجهاز ليقيسو بيه الدم

ill / healthy

مريض / صحيح

alarm

لاارم

assault

يتعدا

Help!

سلكوني

attack

يهجم

danger

دونجي

emergency exit

مخرج الطوارئ

Fire!

النار شاعلة

fire extinguisher

لكستانتور

accident

اكسيدون

first-aid kit

فيزة تاع الاسعاف الاولى

SOS

سلكونا

police

لابوليس

Europe

أوروبا

North America

أمريكا الشمالية

South America

أمريكا الجنوبية

Africa

أفريقيا

Asia

آسيا

Australia

أستراليا

Atlantic

المحيط الأطلسي

Pacific

المحيط الهادي

Indian Ocean

المحيط الهندي

Antarctic Ocean

المحيط المتجمد الجنوبي

Arctic Ocean

المحيط المتجمد الشمالي

North pole

القطب الشمالي

South pole

القطب الجنوبي

Antarctica

منطقة القطب الجنوبي

earth

أرض

land

بلاد

sea

بحر

island

جزيرة

nation

امة

state

دولة

clock face

ميناء الساعة

hour hand

عقرب الساعات

minute hand

عقرب الدقائق

second hand

عقرب الثواني

What time is it?

شعال راها الساعة؟

day

يوم

time

زمن

now

دروك

digital watch

ساعة رقمية

minute

دقيقة

hour

ساعة

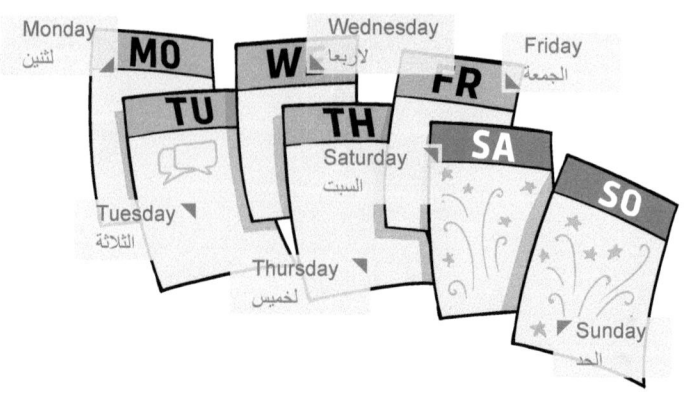

Monday — لثنين
Tuesday — الثلاثة
Wednesday — لاربعا
Thursday — لخميس
Friday — الجمعة
Saturday — السبت
Sunday — لحد

yesterday

لبارح

today

اليوم

tomorrow

غدوا

morning

صباح

noon

القايلة

evening

العشية

workdays

يامات الخدمة

weekend

ويكاند

rain
النو

rainbow
قوس قزح

snow
ثلج

wind
الريح

spring
الربيع

fall
الخريف

summer
الصيف

winter
الشتا

weather forecast
يتنبأ بالحال

thermometer
مقياس حرارة

sunshine
ضوء الشمس

cloud
سحابة

fog
ضباب

humidity
ميديتي

lightning

برق

thunder

رعد

storm

عاصفة

hail

بَرَد

monsoon

ريح

flood

طوفان

ice

جليد

January

جانفي

February

فيفري

March

مارس

April

افريل

May

ماي

June

جوان

July

جويلية

August

اوت

September

سبتمبر

October

اكتوبر

November

نوفمبر

December

ديسمبر

shapes

فورما

circle

دويرة

square

مربع

rectangle

مستطيل

triangle

مثلث

sphere

كويرة

cube

مكعب

white

بيض

yellow

صفر

orange

تٌبيني

pink

روز

red

حمر

purple

حلحالي

blue

زرقَ

green

خظر

brown

قهوري

gray

قري

black

كحل

a lot / a little

بزاف / شوية

angry / calm

زعفان / مكالمي

beautiful / ugly

شباب / مشي شباب

beginning / end

البدية / التالي

big / small

كبير / صغير

bright / dark

فاتح / فونسي

brother / sister

خو / خت

clean / dirty

نقي / موسخ

complete / incomplete

كامل / ناقص

day / night

نهار / الليل

dead / alive

ميت / حي

wide / narrow

عريض / ضيق

edible / inedible

يقدو ياكلوه / ميقدروش ياكلوه

evil / kind

شرير / ناس ملاح

excited / bored

يثير / يمل

fat / thin

سمين / رقيق

first / last

اللولا / التالية

friend / enemy

الصاحب / لعدو

full / empty

معمر / فارغ

hard / soft

قاصح / سويل

heavy / light

ثقيل / خفيف

hunger / thirst

جوع / عطش

ill / healthy

مريض / صحيح

illegal / legal

غير شرعي / شرعي

intelligent / stupid

ذكي / مبوقل

left / right

يسار / يمين

near / far

قريب / بعيد

new / used

جديد / مستعمل

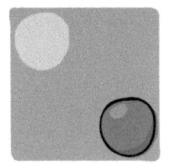

nothing / something

مكانش / شوية

old / young

ثيباني / شاب

on / off

يشعل / يطفئ

open / closed

محلول / مبلع

quiet / loud

بشوية / بلفور

rich / poor

مرفح / زوالي

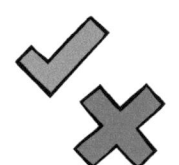

right / wrong

نيشان / خاطيء

rough / smooth

حرش / رطب

sad / happy

زعفان / فرحان

short / long

قصير / طويل

slow / fast

بشوية / بلخف

wet / dry

مشمخ / ناشف

warm / cool

حامي / بارد

war / peace

القيرة / لامان

0	1	2
zero	one	two
صفر	واحد	زوج

3	4	5
three	four	five
ثلاثة	ربعة	خمسة

6	7	8
six	seven	eight
ستة	سبعة	ثمانية

9	10	11
nine	ten	eleven
تسعة	عشرة	حداعش

12
twelve
ثناعش

13
thirteen
تلطاعش

14
fourteen
رباطاعش

15
fifteen
خمسطاعش

16
sixteen
سطاعش

17
seventeen
سبعطَعش

18
eighteen
ثمنطاعش

19
nineteen
تساعطاش

20
twenty
عشرون

100
hundred
مية

1.000
thousand
ألف

1.000.000
million
مليون

English
انقلي

American English
انغلي تاع مريكان

Chinese Mandarin
لغة الشنوية

Hindi
الهندية

Spanish
سبنيولية

French
الفرونسي

Arabic
العربية

Russian
الروسية

Portuguese
البوتغالية

Bengali
البنغالية

German
لالمنية

Japanese
الجابونية

I

انا

you

نتا

he / she / it

هو

we

حنايا

you

نتوما

they

هوما

who?

شكون

what?

واش

how?

كيفاش

where?

وين

when?

وقتاش

name

الاسم

behind

مرول

in

في

in front of

قدام

over

فوق

on

على

under

تحت

beside

حدا

between

بين

place

بلاصة